Doodle and the Magic Pebble
A Story of Courage

Wendy Maybee

Copyright © 2021 by Wendy Maybee
All rights reserved. No part of this book may be reproduced or used in any manner without written permission of the copyright owners except for the use of quotations in a book review or for educational purposes.

Meet Doodle. Doodle was a strong girl who knew how to take care of herself. However, sometimes she worried about things that were new to her. She had a knack for thinking up every what-if for any situation, particularly the worst-case scenario! You could always tell when Doodle was worried because she'd nibble on her fingernails or fiddle with her hair. That was how she got the nickname Doodle!

Doodle tried to avoid anything that made her nervous, even fun things like summer camp. But deep down, she didn't like worrying so much. She didn't want to miss out on fun things. Though she didn't know it, Doodle was about to discover something that would help her see things differently.

One day, Doodle was curled up in the family room, staring out the window. Nana, who was visiting, glanced over and asked, "Doodle, what's spinning around up there in your head?"

"It's about my new school," Doodle said. "I don't know anyone in my class. What if no one talks to me? What if I have to play alone on the playground?" Her voice got higher and louder. "What if I get lost? And what if the *worst thing ever* happens, I freeze in front of class at sharing time, and everyone laughs!"

Nana said, "I can understand why you might be worried, dear. We all have worries, and we all feel uncomfortable at times. But those feelings are temporary. They will pass."

Doodle looked down. She wanted Nana's words to be true, but she just wasn't sure.

"Think of it as an adventure!" Nana said. "That sounds fun, doesn't it? Besides, what's the worst that can happen? Whatever it is, it's part of the adventure and I know you can handle it."

"Well," Doodle replied, "not if I end up all alone, with no one to play with, and never leave my desk!"

Nana walked over and put her arm around Doodle's shoulder. "Let me show you something."

Doodle followed Nana through the kitchen and out the back door. They walked over a curved path to a garden pond. "There is something magical in this pond," Nana whispered. "Can you find it?"

Doodle's eyes got wide. "Magical?" she repeated.

"Yes," said Nana.

Doodle moved next to the pond and leaned over, squinting to see beyond her reflection. She scanned the rock-covered bottom for something unusual. Suddenly, she noticed a single white pebble against the gray backdrop. "Is that it?" Doodle asked.

"What do you see?" asked Nana.

"It's a white pebble, right down there."

"Ah," said Nana. "Yes, that's the one." Nana scooped up the tiny white rock, dabbed it dry on her sleeve, and gently placed it in Doodle's hand.

"How is it magic, Nana?"

"This is a very special pebble," explained Nana. "It finds worries, and like a magnet, it draws them in. It pulls worries away so you aren't bothered by them anymore."

"What do I do with it?" asked Doodle.

"I suppose you should keep it with you," said Nana. "Perhaps in a pocket. Or your shoe."

"I'll put it in my shoe!" exclaimed Doodle.

Doodle took off her shoe and placed the little pebble inside, sliding it to the very end. Then she put the shoe back on and wiggled her big toe. She felt the pebble roll back and forth.

When Doodle stood up, her shoulders shifted back a bit as if a weight had been lifted. "I think it's working already, Nana!" She smiled and took Nana's hand, and they returned to the house.

The next day, Doodle went to school. A teacher greeted her at the entrance and took her to her new classroom. Doodle slowed as she approached the door. The air went quickly in and out of her lungs. She stretched her toes to feel the pebble in her shoe. Her breathing eased. She swallowed and continued inside.

Doodle looked around. She didn't recognize anyone. She sat down at the desk with her name on it and put her backpack on the floor. Other kids were leaning over their desks talking and chattering in groups sprinkled around the room. Doodle felt alone. She began to worry no one would talk to her and started to fidget with her fingers.

Then she caught herself. *Wait*, she thought. *I don't need to worry. I've got the magic pebble.* She pulled herself up out of her chair and made her way to some students huddled by the art table. Her face felt warm, but she pressed on.

"Hi," she said. "I'm Doodle. What are your names?" The children introduced themselves, and the conversation quickly turned to drawing rainbows. *Wow*, Doodle thought. *The magic pebble works!*

Later that day, her class went outside for recess. Doodle walked over to the swings by herself. After a while, she felt lonely. She looked around at other children giggling together. She wanted to join them but worried no one wanted to play with her. She sat cross-legged on the ground and began twisting the hair next to her ear.

She was interrupted by a bouncy ball that landed next to her. When she stood up to return it, the tiny pebble rolled under her foot.

"Ouch," she said. Then she remembered, *the magic pebble!* Doodle noticed another girl sitting alone nearby. She walked over and asked, "Would you like to swing with me?"

"Yes!" replied the girl. "Let's see who can go the highest!"

The girls went from the swings to the monkey bars to the sandbox, where they took off their shoes and socks to build a volcano. They were having so much fun they didn't notice recess had ended. A teacher called to them, waving them back inside. Doodle and her new friend quickly put their shoes on, made their way across the playground, and walked into the school.

But when they got inside, no one was in the hallway. They paused, eyes searching the line of blue doors along each wall. They all looked the same! Doodle and her friend turned to each other, realizing neither one knew which door led to their classroom. Doodle started to worry and felt her body stiffen.

Then she looked over and noticed the girl's eyes were glossy and her lip was quivering. Doodle managed a smile. "Don't worry. What's the worst that can happen?"

The corners of the girl's mouth lifted slightly, and Doodle took her hand. "Let's go. It will be an adventure!" They opened each door one by one until they found their class.

The last part of the school day was reserved for show-and-tell. Each student took a turn sharing at the front of the class. Doodle waited anxiously, holding her breath each time the teacher called the next name. Her stomach ached and her head felt heavy.

Just then, the girl she met on the playground walked past her desk and mouthed, Thank you. Doodle thought about Nana's advice she had shared with her friend. "What's the worst that can happen?" she repeated.

Doodle knew then—she had to let the worry go. If I don't do this, she thought, I won't get to show everyone the pebble and tell them about its magic.

Finally, Doodle's name was called. She closed her eyes, exhaled, and walked to the front of the classroom. "Hello, my name is Doodle, and I'm sharing a special white pebble my nana gave me. It's magic!"

She continued, "I used to worry—*a lot*. I didn't want to try new things. But the magic pebble takes my worries away. Without it, I wouldn't be standing up here."

She thought about the events of the day. "I would have been too worried to meet new friends, too worried to ask someone to play with me, and so worried about getting lost I wouldn't have found my way back to class."

One of the boys asked, "Can we see the magic pebble?"

"Oh, sure," replied Doodle. She bent over to retrieve the pebble from her shoe, but when she looked inside, it wasn't there. She paused to retrace her steps. *It must have fallen out at the sandbox when I took off my shoes*, she thought. Doodle stood up slowly and told the class the pebble was lost.

At that moment, looking out at all those faces from the front of the room, Doodle realized the "worst thing" she could imagine was happening right now.

And yet, she didn't feel worried, she didn't freeze, and no one was laughing at her. She was doing it *without* the magic pebble.

Doodle let the realization sink in, then said, "Maybe the *real* magic of the pebble was showing me I don't need a magic pebble at all. I already have everything I need inside me to handle my worries!" Doodle smiled, and the class applauded.

Doodle always remembered that day as the day she found the courage to face her worries. And every day after, she looked forward to her next adventure!